THE NATION

A Study in Ideology and Fantasy

THE NATION

A Study in Ideology and Fantasy

Richard A. Koenigsberg

IAP

INFORMATION AGE PUBLISHING, INC.

Charlotte, NC • www.infoagepub.com

ISBN: 978-1-59311-857-0

Printed and bound by CPI Group (UK) Ltd, Croydon, CR0 4YY

TABLE OF CONTENTS

Chapter I

THE COUNTRY, THE MOTHER, AND INFANTILE NARCISSISM

1. Introduction

One may view the idea of the nation as a fundamental "assumption" which defines the manner in which modern man perceives, and experiences, social reality. Thus, just as persons in earlier historical periods tended to possess an absolute faith in the reality of God, so, we may suggest, do persons in contemporary cultures tend to possess an *absolute faith in the reality of the nation*.

In a democratic culture, for example, persons commonly differ with respect to the *stance* which is taken in relation to the nation: the country may be "loved" or hated; perceived to be "healthy" or sick; "strong" or weak. But whatever stance is adopted, persons are united within the framework of the culture of nationalism, it would appear, by their *absolute faith in the reality of this entity*, and by their belief that this entity constitutes a fundamental determinant of the nature, and of the quality, of their daily lives.

It is our view that an ideology tends to be embraced and perpetuated, tends to attain a degree of "power" as an element of human culture, insofar as it is able to provide a "modus operandi" for the expression and discharge of phantasies which are shared by human beings. One of the central tasks of the present work, therefore, shall be to attempt to uncover the *nature of the unconscious phantasies which define and sustain the ideology of nationalism*.

In this Chapter, we shall focus upon three *core phantasies*, which may be conceptualized as follows: the phantasy of the nation as a *suffering mother*; the phantasy of the nation as an *omnipotent mother*; the nation as a *projection of infantile narcissism*.[1]

2. The Country as a Suffering Mother

An idea which appears with great frequency throughout the history of nationalism, and of revolution, is the belief that the nation, or that the citizens of the nation, are "suffering." It follows, given such a perception, that an effort must be made to "save the people," that is, to "lift them up" from out of a condition of misery and degradation, and to "improve their condition."

The posture of the nationalist/revolutionary, therefore, we may suggest, may be described as a tendency toward *identification with the suffering masses*: as the people suffer, so does the nationalist/revolutionary suffer with them. Thus Hitler states, typically:

> There are thousands who with bleeding heart feel the misfortune of their people.
>
> (1962, p. 116)

[1] These phantasies would appear to be bound together as part of a dynamic constellation. For purposes of analysis, however, we have treated them as separate entities.

And Michelet expresses the classic posture:

> I have also suffered more. The trials of my childhood are ever present to me; I have never lost the impression of my hard working days, of a harsh, laborious way of life–I am still one of the people.
>
> (1846, p. 23)

The nationalist/revolutionary does not believe, however, that the suffering of the people is inevitable, nor permanent. Rather, he tends to believe that it is possible for the people to be "relieved" of their suffering; and embraces, therefore, as the mission of his life, the struggle to "save" the people. Thus, typically, Mao:

> The Chinese people are suffering; it is our duty to save them and we must exert ourselves in struggle.
>
> (1971, p. 311)

August Kubizek describes Hitler:

> It was not sympathy, in the ordinary sense, he felt for the disinherited. That would not have been sufficient. He not only suffered with them, he lived for them and devoted all his thoughts to the salvation of these people from distress and poverty.
>
> (1954, p. 27)

And Clara Zetlin describes Lenin upon the occasion of their meeting in 1919:

> An expression of unspoken and unspeakable suffering was on his face . . . In my mind I saw the picture of a crucified Christ of the medieval master Grunewald . . .Grunewald's Christ is the martyr, the tortured man, cruelly done to death, who "carries the sins of the world." And as such a "man of sorrows" Lenin appeared to me, burdened, oppressed with all the pain and all the suffering of the Russian working people.
>
> (quoted in Payne, 1967, p. 550)

The revolutionary does, indeed, bear a resemblance to Christ: he embraces the suffering of the great mass of people as his own, and wishes to be their "savior."

The image of the *suffering nation* is expressed, quite frequently, in more specific terms: in the image of a *suffering woman*. Thus, according to Kohn (1944), in one of the first expressions of the idea of nationalism, Alain Chartier (writing in 1422)

> envisioned France in her desolation as a beautiful and royal lady, with the strain of suffering visible on her face and brow and a pitiful disorder in her apparel, contemplating her three children, the nobleman, the cleric, and the peasant, the last of these showing his misery and privations. "Le povre Peuple allegue des doleances et injures à sa mère Dame France, qui luy font souffrir les pillars gens d'armeaulx sous umbre de deffendre la chose publicque." The mutual recriminations and complaints of the three children end in an exhortation to unite for the salvation of the common mother, suffering France.
>
> (p. 114)

Petrarch, in another early expression of nationalism, writes:

> My Italy, though words do not avail
> To heal the mortal wounds
> That in your lovely body I see so dense,
> I wish at least to let my sighing sounds
> With Arno and Tiber wail.
>
> (1968, p. 203)

And Michelet describes the condition of France:

> Behold our poor France, seated on the ground like Job, with her friends, the nations, coming to comfort, question, improve her if they can, and labor at her salvation . . . Kind sisters, who thus come to comfort France, permit me to answer you. She is ill, you see; and there she sits with drooping head, unwilling to speak.
>
> (1846, p. 168)

Here, then, are certain beliefs, and certain patterns of imagery, which appear early in the history of nationalism, and which are reiterated to the present day: the belief that the nation is "sick," or that it has been "wounded;" the belief that the citizens of the nation are "suffering;" and the belief that it is the duty of the nationalist, consequently, to take steps in order to "save the nation" or to "relieve the suffering of the people." The question is, therefore: How may we account for the recurrence of these beliefs and patterns of imagery?

Without becoming involved in a detailed discussion of the theoretical issues relating to this question, I wish, merely, to state the following hypothesis: the nature of the recurring patterns of imagery which appear in relation to the overt elements of an ideology constitutes data which permits one to ascertain the nature of the *latent or unconscious meaning of the ideology*.

In light of this hypothesis I wish to attempt to reconstruct here, in a speculative way, the unconscious meaning of the patterns of belief which have been described in this section.

Firstly: the tendency toward an *identification with the suffering masses* reflects, we may suggest, the wish to be *united with the mother in a bond of shared suffering*. The nationalist/revolutionary, according to this view, is an individual who *refuses to separate from the mother*, and who expresses this refusal in the form of his tendency to cling to a symbol of the mother, "the people."[2]

Secondly: the image of a nation which is "sick" or "dying" symbolizes, we may hypothesize, the image of the *idealized mother in a state of deterioration*. What is "dying,"

[2]Hitler, in this context, states: "Man today . . . will bear extreme distress and misery, but he desires to remain with his people (Baynes, 1942, p. 1438)."

in other words, when the nation is perceived to be dying, is the *belief in the omnipotence of the mother*, the belief in the absolute quality of her "goodness," "power," "beauty," etc.

It follows, according to this view, that the wish to "save the nation" is the projective equivalent of the wish to *restore the omnipotence of the mother*: the nationalist aspires to help the mother/country to recover her "goodness," "beauty," "power," etc., and, in so doing, to make her worthy of his continued devotion.

3. The Country as an Omnipotent Mother

I wish, here, to present several passages from the writings of Michelet and Aurobindo which depict the nation in the image of an *omnipotent mother*.

Michelet, in the following passage, describes the French nation as

> a living person which the child touches and feels on every side. He cannot embrace her, but she embraces him, warms him with her great soul diffused throughout that multitude, and speaks to him by her monuments.
>
> (1846, p. 180)

And suggests that the citizens of the nation should

> (let France be) thy first Gospel, the stay of thy life, the food of thy heart. Thou wilt dwell upon it when toiling at the painful, ungrateful tasks to which the world will summon thee. It will be a powerful cordial to revive thee when thy spirit faints within thee. It will beguile thee thoughts during the long days of labor, and deadly wearisomeness of manufacturing life. In the desert of Africa thou wilt meet with it to cheer thy homesick heart; to sustain thee when worn out by marchings and

watchings, standing sentinel at the advance post, two steps from the barbarians.

(1846, pp. 182–183)

As a "living person" which "embraces and warms" the individual, the nation may be characterized, then, as a *protective mother*:

> (The citizen of a nation should) not only see and learn his country, but feel her as Providence, recognize her as mother and as nurse, by her strengthening milk and vivifying warmth.
>
> (Michelet, 1846, p. 181)

> If thou are naked and hungry, hither, my son; the gates are wide open, and France on the threshold with open arms to receive thee. Never will this great mother be ashamed to attend thee as nurse; with her own heroic hand will she make thee the soldier's soup.
>
> (Michelet, 1846, p. 182)

As a mother which is *shared in common* by the citizens of the nation:

> We have all one common mother,–men, women, children, animals, plants, all that has life,–a tender mother who always feeds us, and is invisible yet present . . . Let us love her, dear child, let us embrace her with all our heart.
>
> (Michelet, 1846, p. 179)

> There is one place in which you all meet and that is your common Mother . . . That is not merely a division of land but it is a living thing. It is the Mother in whom you move and have your being.
>
> (Aurobindo, 1952a, p. 115)

And as a mother which *embraces and unites* the nation's citizens, as brothers contained within a common womb:

> (The Indian nation is a) mighty association which unites

> the people of East and North Bengal and defies partition, because it embraces every son of the land,—brother and brother massed inseparably together.
>
> (Aurobindo, 1952a, p. 114)

What these passages suggest, then, is that when the image of the omnipotent mother is projected into reality, the environment ceases to be experienced as a cold, "external" territory. Rather, it would appear, under such circumstances, the environment becomes "transformed," and comes to be experienced as a "special place," a place which functions to provide *shelter and protection from the vicissitudes of reality*.

In other words, insofar as the nation is experienced, by the nationalist, as a projection of the omnipotent mother, the nationalist tends to feel that, as long as he is contained within the boundaries of the nation, he shall be *shielded from the external world*: the nation shall act as a "buffer," standing between the individual and the harshness of reality.

The nation, then, it would appear, is experienced as an omnipotent object. This being the case, the nation becomes the object, we may suggest, of the *religious impulse*. I wish, here, to briefly discuss the religious impulse as it is expressed in the ideology of nationalism; to discuss, that is to say, the tendency of the nationalist to *worship the nation as an omnipotent object*.

One of the central distinctions between the religion of nationalism and the Christian religion, we may suggest, is that while the Christian worships an object which is "invisible," the nationalist worships an object which can, in some sense, be "perceived." Thus Fichte describes the nation as a thing "in whose soul heaven and earth, visible and invisible meet and mingle, and thus, and only thus, create a true and enduring heaven (1968, p. 117)."

It is this capacity to combine "visible and invisible" which constitutes, I believe, a fundamental source of the power of the ideology of nationalism. Thus, unlike God, the nation possesses "referents" in the real world: there does, indeed, exist a body of territory; there are human beings who reside within this territory; there are governing institutions which "represent" it.

But the nation is, of course, much more than these "referents" in the external world: it is conceived of, and related to, as a single, integral entity. Thus, we may suggest, a primary function of these referents in the external world is to provide a *"material base" upon which the phantasy of an omnipotent object may be projected.* By citing the existence of a body of territory, of millions of "people," of governing institutions, etc., the nationalist is able to persuade himself that the omnipotent object which he worships is "real," that it exists as a part of the external world.

Modern man believes that he lives in a rational world, and that his central preoccupation is reality. Existing co-extensively with this "profane" world, however, is this "sacred object," the nation. The nation, that is to say, may be viewed as a sacred object which merges with, which "saturates" our day to day reality, as a sacred object which "accompanies us" as we move through our daily activities.

Thus, while modern man finds it difficult to place God in the center of his life, insofar as his "manifestations" are not readily observable, he has no trouble "believing in" the nation: its manifestations are all around him. The Christian deity falls before the empirical spirit: "What is the evidence for the existence of God?" One rarely, however, hears the question: "What is the evidence for the existence of the nation?"

4. The Country as a Projection of Infantile Narcissism

We have presented evidence which suggests, then, that various perceptions of the nation are rooted in the *projection of infantile phantasies into the external world*, phantasies which bring about a transformation in the manner in which reality is experienced.

Thus, in the first case, we argued that the image of the *suffering mother* was projected into reality, giving rise to the belief that the nation was "sick" or "dying." In the second case, we argued that the image of the *omnipotent mother* was projected into reality, giving rise to the belief that the nation could provide *protection against the vicissitudes of reality*. Here, we wish to argue that various perceptions of the nation embody the *projection of the infantile narcissistic ego* into the external world.

The idea of the nation is an embodiment, we may hypothesize, of the *shared narcissism* of an entire group of persons. Thus, according to this view, the belief in the "greatness," "power," "beauty," etc. of the nation arises out of a *people's belief in its own greatness, power, beauty*, etc. The nation, in short, may be viewed as a *symbol of the narcissistic ego*, a narcissistic ego which is *shared in common* by a nation's citizens.[3]

Further, we may suggest, insofar as the nation is a symbol of the narcissistic ego, the nationalist tends to adopt a posture toward the nation which is similar to the posture which he adopts toward his own ego, e.g., he wants it to be "healthy," "strong," "good," etc. What we encounter here, I believe, is a wish which is a fundamental one among nationalists: the wish to *maintain the purity of the nation*.

[3]It follows that the citizens of a nation, in worshipping and glorifying the nation, are worshipping and glorifying themselves: they "bow down" to this projection of their own narcissism.

There is a tendency to associate this wish, the wish to maintain the purity of the nation, with fanatic racist ideologies, e.g., Hitler's wish to "purify" Germany. What we are dealing with here, however, I believe, is a motive which has far broader implications and meanings.

That is to say: the wish to purify the nation is expressed, in my view, *any time a particular condition or situation is identified as the source of the "badness" which exists within the boundaries of the nation*; and any time it is believed that the maintenance or the restoration of the "goodness" of the nation is contingent upon the "removal" of this condition or situation.[4]

It follows, from this point of view, that racism and revolution may be described as *specific strategies* which are undertaken with the purpose of maintaining or restoring the narcissistic goodness of the nation. This strategy takes the form, in each case, of the *identification of a particular class of persons within the boundaries of the nation as the source of the nation's "badness;"* and of the belief that, if the "goodness" of the nation is to be maintained or restored, this particular class of persons must be "removed" from within the nation's boundaries.

[4] Thus, according to this view, the wish to "purify" the nation is expressed, typically: in the desire to eliminate "pollution" from within the environment; in the desire to remove "negative social conditions," such as crime or poverty, from within the boundaries of the nation; in the desire to eliminate "corruption" from within the government.

Chapter II

THE COUNTRY AS A LIVING ORGANISM

1. Racism and Revolution as a Wish to Eliminate the "Disease" from Within the Body of the Nation

An image which is commonly used among nationalists to describe the nation, and among communists to describe the party, is the image of the nation, or the party, as a "living organism." Thus, typically, Hitler:[1]

> From a dead mechanism (the state) there must be formed a living organism.
>
> (1962, p. 398)

Aurobindo:

> (A nation) . . . is an organism which grows under the stress of a principle of life within.
>
> (Mukherjee, 1964, p. 27)

And Stalin:

> Our party is a living organism. Like every organism, it undergoes a process of metabolism: the old and obsolete passes away, the new and growing lives and develops.
>
> (Rigby, 1966, p. 43)

[1]Further examples of Hitler's use of this image appear in *Hitler's Ideology* (Koenigsberg, 1975, pp. 5–6).

Given this conception, the conception of the nation as a living organism, there are a number of propositions which follow logically, and which are frequently put forth by racists and revolutionaries:

(1) The nation or the party is susceptible to *disease*, i.e., to the possibility that germs, infections, cancers, etc., may invade its body, and cause it to become "ill." Thus Mao suggests that self-criticism within the party

> prevents the inroads of germs and other organisms . . . prevents all kinds of political dust and germs from contaminating the minds of our comrades and the body of our Party . . . (We cannot) allow political dust and germs to . . . eat into our healthy organisms.
>
> (1971, p. 317)

(2) The source of the nation's disease may be a *particular class of persons lying within the body of the nation*. Thus, among anti-Semites, we find Lagarde describing the Jews as

> the carriers of decay who pollute every national culture . . . with trichinae and bacilli one does not negotiate . . . they are exterminated as quickly and as thoroughly as possible.
>
> (quoted in Minogue, 1967, p. 78)

And Hitler referring to them as persons who[2]

[2] Similarly, among contemporary anti-Semites, Idi Amin, president of Uganda, compares Israel to "A person with a contagious cancer. Any Arab country that sits at the same table with the Israelis will come down with a disease (quoted in the *New York Post*, June 23, 1975)." While Jamil Baroody, Saudi Arabian representative to the United Nations discusses the problem of Israel as follows: "There will be no peace as long as this foreign element is among us, a festering wound that has caused the abscess and the high fever. And there will be no peace unless the pus is drained from the body politic and the body social of the Arab world (from *A Delegate's Odyssey*, by William F. Buckley, Jr., excerpted in the *New York Post*, December 27, 1974)."

> are suffering from a poisonous infection and who openly profess their desire to infect others with the same disease.
>
> (Baynes, 1942, p. 694)

While among revolutionaries we find Sieyes describing the "privileged class" as

> some horrible disease eating the living flesh on the body of some unfortunate man . . . (it) is a plague for the nation which suffers from it.
>
> (quoted in Minogue, 1967, p. 471)

And Aurobindo depicting India's reaction to British rule as

> the instinctive protest of Nature against the malady that was eating its way into the national system and threatened to corrupt its blood and disturb the soundness of its organs.
>
> (Mukherjee, 1964, p. 356)

(3) In order to achieve a "cure" for the disease from which the nation is suffering, it may be necessary to "remove" a particular class of persons from within the body of the nation, just as a surgeon removes a diseased part of the body whose continued existence is a threat to the survival of the organism.

Thus, according to Lenin:

> The way of reform is the way of delay, of procrastination, of the painfully slow decomposition of the putrid parts of the national organism. It is the proletariat and the peasantry that suffer first of all and most of all from their putrefaction. The revolutionary way is the way of quick amputation, which is the least painful to the proletariat, the way of the direct removal of the decomposing parts.
>
> (1965b, pp. 45-46)

Similarly, the justification of violence which appears in the writing of the Parisian Commune:

> Thus, the clever and helpful surgeon with his cruel and benevolent knife cuts off the gangrened limb in order to save the body of the sick man.
>
> (quoted in Arendt, 1971, p. 8)

Finally Dimitrov, an assistant of Stalin, describes the purge of the mid-thirties in terms of the necessity of "cutting into good flesh in order to get rid of the bad (Djilas, 1962, p. 58)."

What we encounter here, then, it would appear, is a *coherent phantasy*, which may be summarized as follows: the nation is a living organism; this organism is suffering from a "disease," the source of which is a *particular class of persons* lying within the body of this organism; in order to cure this disease, and thereby to "save the nation," it may be necessary to "remove" this class of persons from within the body of the nation.

This phantasy is, in my view, a fundamental source of acts of destruction, and particularly of mass-destruction, which are carried out in the name of racist and revolutionary ideologies: the perpetrators of mass-destruction think of themselves, not as murderers, but as men who have undertaken the "necessary task" of removing a disease element from within the body of the nation.[3]

[3] Or, to put this in somewhat different language (see Chapter I, section 4), the racist and the revolutionary are men who perpetrate acts of destruction in the name of the *purification of the narcissistic ego*. Whether the target of hostility be the Jew, the Negro, the capitalist, or a member of the ruling class, these men are, fundamentally, "exorcists" who believe that the maintenance of the goodness of the nation can be achieved only through the "removal" of a certain class of persons from within the nation's boundaries.

2. The Disease Within the Nation as a Projection of Malignant Internal Objects

The class of persons which is identified as a "disease element," then, may be characterized as a class of persons which lies *within* the boundaries of the nation, but which is perceived, simultaneously, as *not belonging there*. This class of persons, in short, is perceived as an *alien element* within the body of the nation, an element which must be "rejected," just as any other organism rejects alien elements which invade the interior of its body, and which endanger its health.

We may hypothesize further that, insofar as the nation represents a projection of the ego of the nationalist (see Chapter I, section 4), the "alien element" perceived to be lying within the boundaries of the nation represents the projection of an *alien element lying within the boundaries of the ego of the nationalist*. The question is, therefore: What is the nature of this alien element?

The "alien element" lying within the boundaries of the nation represents, we may hypothesize, the projection of a *malignant internal object lying within the boundaries of the ego of the nationalist*. Thus, according to this view, it is the experience of an *alien mental representation* (a mental representation which is perceived as lying *within* the boundaries of the ego, but as *not belonging there*) which gives rise to the perception of an *alien class of persons lying within the boundaries of the nation* (a class of persons which, similarly, is perceived as lying within the boundaries of *the nation*, but as *not belonging there*).

The *disease within the nation*, then, according to the theory presented here, is the *disease of neurosis*. And racism and revolution constitute *modes of psychotherapy*, modes of activity which are undertaken in the struggle for liberation from malignant internal objects.[4]

In the case of Aurobindo, I believe, one may observe the manner in which *intrapsychic perceptions* are transformed into *political perceptions*. Thus, in the following passages, Aurobindo describes the consequences of British rule:

> The central governing body has . . . been either destroyed or crippled by the intrusion of a foreign organism.
>
> (1952a, p. 41)

> The tendency of the intruding body is to break down all the existing organs of national life and to engross all power in itself.
>
> (Mukherjee, 1964, p. 32)

> Foreign rule is unnatural and fatal to a nation precisely because by its very nature it throws itself upon these activities and capacities and crushes them down in the interests of its own continued existence. Even when it does not crush them down violently, it obstructs their growth passively by its very nature. The subject becomes dependent, disorganized and loses its powers by atrophy.
>
> (Mukherjee, 1964, p. 25)

> As soon as the foreign organism begins to dominate the body politic, it compels the whole body to look to it as the centre of its activities and neglects its own organs of action till these become atrophied.
>
> (1952a, p. 41)

[4]This entire tendency toward the "rejection of alien elements" is rooted ultimately, I believe, in the organismic tendency toward the *maintenance of its own narcissistic integrity*: the narcissistic integrity of the *body*; of the *psyche*; and of the *social unit with which one identifies*. One may recall Freud's hypothesis that the perception of one's own ego is derived from perceptions relating to one's own body (i.e., that the human ego is ultimately a *body ego*). One may extend this hypothesis, in light of the present analysis, and suggest that the human perception of *political units* is derived, similarly, from perceptions which are rooted in the perception of one's own body.

What these passages represent, I believe, is an accurate description, in the form of a projection, of the psychological consequences of the *intrapsychic presence of a malignant internal object*. Thus, according to this view, it is Aurobindo's experience of an *intruding organism within his own psyche* which gives rise to his perception of an "intruding organism" within the nation; and it is the *crippling effects* of this internal object upon Aurobindo's own capacity to act and to will which gives rise to his belief that a foreign organism is "crippling the central governing body," "obstructing the growth of the nation's capacities," etc.[5]

According to the theory developed here, then, racism and revolution may be described as the *struggle for liberation from a malignant internal object as waged in the form of a struggle for liberation from an alien class of persons*. Lacking the capacity to wage a struggle against an *intrapsychic oppressor*, the racist and revolutionary wage a struggle against an oppressor in the external world.

[5]What we observe in the case of Aurobindo, I believe, is the underlying psychological process which is the source of the belief, so common among nationalists and revolutionaries (see Chapter III), that the citizens of the nation are suffering from a *disease of the will*.

Chapter III

REVOLUTION AS A STRUGGLE AGAINST PASSIVITY

1. The Struggle Against Passivity: Hitler

The struggle against submission is a central theme in Hitler's ideology. He speaks, in the following passages, in the classic language of revolutionary liberation:

> The world must learn that the time is past when the German people could be oppressed, subjugated, and dishonoured, and, further, that that time will never return.
>
> (Baynes, 1942, p. 1150)

> Come what may, Germany will stand firm, she will not bow, she will never again submit.
>
> (Baynes, 1942, p. 1331)

A struggle against submission is perceived to be necessary, not only because of the existence of external oppressors, but because of the tendency of the German nation toward the adoption of a servile, masochistic posture:

> The state . . . on November 9, 1918, unconditionally crawled on its belly before Marxism.
>
> (Hitler, 1962, p. 535)

> A man couldn't help feeling ashamed to be a German when he saw . . . this wretched licking of France's boots.
>
> (Hitler, 1962, p. 54)

And because of weakness in the German character:

> (The) results (of German education) were not strong men, but compliant "walking encyclopedias."
>
> (1962, p. 237)

> People liked the German because he was easy to make use of, but respected him little, precisely because of his weakness of will.
>
> (1962, p. 237)

As a means of overcoming these tendencies, Hitler enjoins the German people to become "hard:"

> We ask of you to be hard, German youth, and to make yourselves hard! We cannot use a generation of "mother's boys," of spoiled children.
>
> (Baynes, 1942, p. 547)

And to embrace "deeds and perpetual activity:"

> We Germans above all, with our long-established habit of brooding and dreaming to excess, needed to be brought back to the great truth that only deeds and perpetual activity give meaning to life.
>
> (Rauschning, 1940, p. 224)

What these descriptions of the German nation and of the German people represent, I believe, is a *massive projection of Hitler's own intrapsychic situation*, that is, a projection of the weakness and passivity which Hitler experiences within himself. Thus, according to this view, it is Hitler's perception of *his own tendencies toward masochism and submission* which is the source of his belief that the German people are "easy to make use of;" and of his perception that the nation is "crawling on its belly," "licking France's boots," etc.

Further, we may suggest, it is precisely as a response to the perception of his own weakness and passivity that Hitler embraces the "revolutionary struggle." Thus, Hitler's espousal of "hardness" and of "deeds and perpetual activity," his affirmation that Germany shall "never again submit" function, I believe, as ideological stances which permit Hitler to *do battle against his own inclination toward weakness and passivity.*

In the following passages, Hitler expresses his belief in the value of "crime:"

> Every crime in the old sense towers above respectable inactivity. Action may be negative from the viewpoint of the community, and must then be prevented. But it is at least action.
>
> (Rauschning, 1940, p. 224)

> Every deed has its place, even crime. All passivity, all inertia, on the other hand, is senseless and inimical to life.
>
> (Rauschning, 1940, p. 224)

Criminal activities, these passages suggest, are perceived by Hitler to be an important element in the struggle against passivity: such activities are advocated because they are "at least action;" and because they are perceived to be preferable to "respectable inactivity" and to "passivity and inertia."

We may pose, then, the following question: In what sense does participation in criminal activities function as a means of permitting the individual to wage a struggle against passivity?

Participation in criminal activities, i.e., in activities where violence and terrorism play a major role, function, we may hypothesize, for Hitler as well as for other revolutionaries, as a means of permitting the individual to *affirm the power of the will where the power to will is perceived to be precarious.*

That is to say: acts of violence constitute a *direct and concentrated expression of the active will*; acts of violence, however negative their consequences, are undeniably *action*. As such, acts of violence function, I believe, as a mode of activity which permits the individual to *do battle against his inclinations toward passivity and inertia.*

Criminal activities, then, according to this theory, are an important element of the revolutionary struggle by virtue of their inherent character as modes of activity. We may suggest, however, an additional hypothesis: that such activities play a central role in the revolutionary struggle by virtue of their *psychological meaning*. Specifically, we wish to argue that participation in such activities constitutes the means by which the individual *wages a struggle against the super-ego.*

We suggested earlier (Chapter II, section 2) that an important source of the sense of weakness and passivity is the psychic presence of a *malignant internal object*, a mental representation which acts to "cripple" the individual in his efforts to act and to will.

If we identify this malignant internal object as the *super-ego* we broaden our understanding of its inhibitory power: it acts to create a sense of passivity, not merely by virtue of its "intrusive presence," but by virtue of the fact that it embodies certain *moral codes and strictures* which limit the range of acceptable modes of behavior.

It follows, therefore, that participation in criminal activities functions to permit the individual to *rebel* against the super-ego; functions to permit the individual to *wage a struggle against that psychic structure which is perceived to be the source of his weakness and passivity*. By embracing activities which are illegal, and which are morally condemned, the revolutionary affirms, I believe, a *refusal to be bound by the dictates of the super-ego*: affirms a refusal to permit this internal object to regulate his activities *vis a vis* the external world.

For Hitler, this aspect of the revoluntionary struggle, the struggle against morality and the super-ego, would appear to have been clearly perceived. Thus, in the following passage, Hitler describes his "mission:"

> Providence has ordained that I should be the greatest liberator of humanity. I am freeing men from the restraints of an intelligence that has taken charge; from the dirty and degrading self-mortifications of a chimera called conscience and morality.
> (Rauschning, 1940, p. 225)

Hitler believes, apparently, that for his generation, the older generation, the struggle for liberation from the "dirty and degrading self-mortifications of conscience" is futile, insofar as the sense of servility has become too deeply engrained:

> We older ones are used up. Yes, we are old already. We are rotten to the marrow. We have no unrestrained instincts left. We are cowardly and sentimental. We are bearing the burden of a humiliating past, and have in our blood the dull recollection of serfdom and servility.
> (Rauschning, 1940, p. 251)

It is upon the German youth, therefore, that Hitler focuses his educative work:

> But my magnificent youngsters! Are there finer ones anywhere in the world? Look at these young men and boys! What material! With them I can make a new world.
> (Rauschning, 1940, p. 251)

> I want to see once more in its eyes the gleam of pride and independence of the beast of prey. Strong and handsome must my young men be. I will have them fully trained in all physical

> exercises. I intend to have an athletic young—that is the first and the chief thing. In this way I shall eradicate the thousands of years of human domestication. Then I shall have in front of me the pure and noble natural material. With that I can create the new order.
>
> (Rauschning, 1940, p. 252)

What these passages suggest, then, is that Hitler aspired to *liberate the German people, and humanity, from the burden of conscience*. By eradicating "thousands of years of human domestication" Hitler hoped to create a "new order," a race of men who would be free from the oppressive burden of the super-ego.

We may conclude, then, on the basis of this analysis, that a central element of the revolutionary struggle is the *struggle for liberation from the super-ego*. In embracing activities which are illegal, and which are morally condemned, the revolutionary, it would appear, is acting in a manner such that he may *directly confront his oppressor*; is acting in a manner, in short, which permits him to *oppose* the dictates of that psychic structure which is perceived to be the source of his weakness.

2. The Struggle Against Passivity: Lenin

At the heart of Lenin's revolutionary posture lies a commitment to *total revolution*; a commitment, that is to say, to the *absolute destruction of the enemy*. This being the case, Lenin exhibits intense hostility and contempt toward persons who express a willingness to *compromise* with the enemy; toward persons whose commitment to revolution is less than absolute.

And the class of persons which is the prime target of Lenin's hostility and contempt, in this regard, is the "intellectual." Lenin exhibits throughout his life, as Frank observes, "A fierce hatred of the intelligentsia, a withering contempt for its lack of fibre and sentimentality (in Schapiro, 1967, p. 31)."[1]

Lenin's hostility toward the intellectual would appear to be linked with his perception of the intellectual as a person who was *incapable of acting in a decisive manner*; with his perception of the intellectual as a person who, though capable of *theorizing* about revolution, tended to "waver" when confronted with the necessity for decisive revolutionary action.

Lenin's attitude toward the intellectual leads us, I believe, to the core of his psychology. It is worthwhile to examine, therefore, in general terms, the relationship between the revolutionary posture and the posture of the intellectual.

The revolutionary may be characterized, in contrast to other "men of action" (e.g., the entrepreneur), by his tendency to place a great deal of value upon abstract ideas and upon theoretical concepts. It is important, for the revolutionary, that his actions be consistent with his ideas, that his behavior follow in the path which is dictated by his ideology.

Further, the revolutionary quite frequently *is* an intellectual: a man who places a great deal of value upon books and ideas. Marx is famous, not only for his theories, but for the amount of time he spent in libraries. And Lenin, in spite of his contempt for intellectuals, was a prolific reader (see Payne, 1967, p. 488) and a prolific writer (his *Collected Works*, in the English edition, occupy forty-five volumes averaging approximately five-hundred pages each).

[1]Thus we find Lenin speaking, typically, in his writings and conversation of the "spineless intellectual (Valentinov, 1968, p. 126);" the "wishy-washy intellectual (Valentinov, 1968, p. 126);" of "intellectualist impotence (Lenin, 1962a, p. 283);" and of the "whining intellectual trash (Lenin, 1962b, p. 381)."

For the revolutionary, however, a commitment to ideas is not sufficient: one must be committed, rather, in addition, to the *activation of one's ideas in reality.*[2]

It follows, therefore, that the posture of the intellectual may be an *anti-revolutionary posture*, insofar as the intellectual's attachment to *words and ideas* may diminish the intensity of his commitment to *action.*

And this, in fact, is the position taken by Lenin: that the intellectual's attachment to *words and ideas*, that his over-involvement with the *theory* of revolution, is the source of his inability to wage revolution in an effective manner; and is the source, more generally, of his tendency to be rendered impotent by the tasks posed by reality.[3]

What we encounter in the person of Lenin, then, is the paradox of a man who is a prolific reader and writer, a man who spends a large portion of his life engaging in polemics and debates, yet who nevertheless expresses a virulent hostility and contempt toward intellectuals. The question is, therefore: How may we account for this attitude?

Lenin's hostility toward the intellectual reflects, we may hypothesize, the *hostility which Lenin experiences toward the intellectual within himself*, that is to say, the hostility which Lenin experiences toward that part of himself which tends toward an *overvaluation of words and ideas*, and towards a *devaluation of reality and action*. As Frank observes:

[2]Thus Lenin states, typically, that "Marxism without appropriate deeds is nothing—only words, words, and more words (quoted in Valentinov, 1968, p. 127)."

[3]Thus we find Lenin attributing the ineffectiveness of his political opponents, typically, to the fact that they are "unable to see real life from behind the dusty pages of bourgeois books (1965a, p. 27);" and to their tendency to engage in "soulless and lifeless 'philosophizing' (1965b, p. 106)."

> (People) hate others because they see in them a reflection of their own defects. It would not be far-fetched to surmise that Lenin hated and despised the intelligentsia because he saw in them something that he was determined to root out of himself—sentimentality, self-delusion, political flabbiness.
>
> (in Schapiro, 1967, p. 31)

The intellectual, according to this view, is a *symbol of weakness and passivity*, a symbol of the weakness and passivity which Lenin experiences within himself. And Lenin's rage against the intellectual, therefore, represents an *externalization of Lenin's rage against his own weakness and passivity*: Lenin "does battle" against weakness by waging war against the intellectual.

Lenin's war against the intellectual is, however, I believe, only one aspect of the war which Lenin wages against weakness and passivity. I wish to argue, here, that this war lies, as well, at the heart of Lenin's struggle against the capitalist.

An image which appears throughout Lenin's writings as a description of the state, and of the capitalist, is that of a *parasite*. Thus Lenin speaks, typically, of a "*parasitic organism* (1970, p. 34)" which wishes to "suck the blood of the people (1965a, p. 64);" and which wishes to "devour all the forces of society (1970, p. 13)." The capitalist is visualized by Lenin, in short, in the image of an organism which survives by *devouring the substance of another living organism.*

The idea of the *parasitic capitalist*, therefore, we may suggest, is bound up with the idea of *exploitation*. An exploiter, that is to say, like a parasite, is, for Lenin, an individual who wishes to *use the productive energies of other persons as the means for survival*, but who does not wish, himself, to make a productive contribution.[4]

[4]Thus Lenin describes capitalists, typically, in contrast to workers, as "Persons who are not at labor in (the oil) industry but who try to live off it without labor, by speculation, by royalties, by investment unaccompanied by work of daily toil (quoted in Payne, 1967, p. 429)."

We hypothesized earlier (see Chapter II, section 2) that one might view the idea of the nation as a *projection of the ego of the nationalist*. Extending this hypothesis, and applying it to the case of Lenin, we may suggest that Lenin's perception of a *parasite which is sucking the blood of the people* represents a projection of Lenin's perception of a *parasite which is attached to his own ego, and which is sucking its blood*. The question becomes, therefore: What is the nature of this intrapsychic parasite?

The *parasite which is sucking the blood of the people* represents, we may theorize, a *projection of Lenin's oral-passive self*, that is, a projection of that part of Lenin which remains infantile, and which wishes to "live off" other persons. It follows that the struggle which Lenin wages against the capitalist/exploiter/parasite represents an *externalization of Lenin's struggle against the parasite within himself*, an externalization of the struggle which Lenin wages against his own oral-passive tendencies.

From Lenin's point of view, then, it would appear, there is a commonality between the intellectual and the capitalist: just as the intellectual is perceived to prefer the *passive contemplation of reality to the active encounter with reality*, so does Lenin believe that the capitalist prefers to *passively depend upon the productive activity of other persons* rather than to become involved, himself, in productive activities. Each of these classes of persons constitutes, in short, for Lenin, a *symbol of passivity*, a symbol of the withdrawal from reality and from the active participation in life.

Let us turn, now, to another line of evidence which supports the view that the revolutionary struggle represented, for Lenin, a struggle against passivity.

One of the most important influences upon the young Lenin, according to a number of observers (e.g., Valentinov,

1969; Haimson, 1967), was the Russian writer, Dobrolyubov. Valentinov, who was personally acquainted with Lenin, reports that Lenin often recalled the impression which one of Dobrolyubov's critical essays had made upon him. Let us present, here, Valentinov's summary of this essay:[5]

> Dobrolyubov took aim at Oblomov, the main character of Goncharov's novel . . . and made an extensive survey of the state and condition of Russian society . . . Oblomovka is Russia; it is "an all-absorbing, unconquerable slumber, a true likeness of death," the kingdom of stagnant peace, quiet, and inaction . . . This pernicious spirit permeated Oblomov during his childhood and as he grew up, killed his natural liveliness, and infected him forever with a lazy and comfortable drowsiness. There were moments when Oblomov displayed a keen and clear mind, when he was seized by a desire for action, when he wanted to be active, when he made far-reaching plans, but everything died out quickly. He again lay on the sofa in his dressing-gown and all his dreams came to nothing. And thus went his life. *"I understand everything, but I do not have any strength or will."* Dobrolyubov passionately hated the weak-willed, powerless Oblomov-like Russia, caught in the sleepy drowsiness of a slave and lying humbly and obediently under the heel of the autocratic tsar. He . . . looked at the phenomenon of *Oblomovshchina* as a disease of the national psychology . . . The people who grew up on Russian soil were regarded by Dobrolyubov as idlers, incapable of either a protest or struggle, as weak-willed, "superfluous" nonentities . . . "Oblomovka," he exclaimed in anger, "is our real native land! There is a part of Oblomov in every one of us. Who will liberate us from this torpid stagnation and peace?"
>
> (1969, pp. 198–199)

Lenin read this essay in 1888, and, according to Valentinov:

[5]This essay is entitled "Chto takoe Oblomovschina?" ("What is Oblomovschina?"), and appeared in the journal *Sovremennik* in 1859.

> Dobrolyubov's glorification of will struck a responsive chord in the strong-willed personality of Vladimir Ulyanov. It awakened and nourished in him the thought at that time that he would be the one who would throw out to Oblomovian Russia the all-powerful word "Forward!" The hated image of Oblomov, in all of its numerous personality types engraved itself deeply into the brain of Lenin.
>
> (1969, p. 199)

Haimson, in his study of the origins of Bolshevism, makes a similar observation:

> Just as Chernyshevskii and Dobrolyubov, Lenin would consider it his mission to fight against Oblomovism, to combat the somnolence, the apathy, the inclination to live by dreams rather than by action, which he ascribed to the Russian "national psychology."
>
> (1967, p. 101)

And Valentinov reports, finally, that the following words were ascribed to Lenin: "The mission of my life is to struggle against Oblomov (1969, p. 201)."

The evidence presented here strongly supports the view, then, that the revolutionary struggle constituted for Lenin, as it did for Hitler, an *affirmation of the power of the will in the struggle against passivity*: Lenin, like so many other nationalists and revolutionaries, believes that his fellow-countrymen are suffering from the disease of *weakness of the will*; and he encourages them to embrace the revolutionary struggle as a means of *strengthening* the will; as a means of conquering the inclination toward passivity.

It would appear, however, that in spite of a lifetime of revolutionary activity, Lenin feels that neither he, nor the Russian people, have been successful in conquering this tendency. In a speech delivered in 1922 Lenin states:

> There was such a Russian type—Oblomov. He lay on his bed

> all the time and made up plans. Many years have passed. Russia has undergone three revolutions, and yet the Oblomovs remain . . . The old Oblomov has remained (with us), and we must wash him, cleanse him, shake him and thrash him, in order to get some sense out of him.
>
> (quoted in Haimson, 1969, p. 101)

Thus, according to Lenin, in spite of three revolutions, the "old Oblomov," Russian passivity, remains.

Let us use the preceding passage as the basis for some concluding speculative remarks.

Lenin's desire to "shake and to thrash the old Oblomov" is equivalent, we may suggest, to Lenin's desire to destroy "parasites." That is to say: the struggle against "Oblomov" is Lenin's struggle against weakness and passivity as he perceives it *within himself and within the Russian people*; whereas the struggle against "parasites" is Lenin's struggle against weakness and passivity as he perceives it *in the form of a projection*.

Further, we may speculate, the need to destroy "parasites" arises, for Lenin, when the *internal struggle to control his own weakness and passivity becomes too much of a burden*. According to this view, Lenin seeks to relieve internal psychological pressures, on these occasions, by means of an *externalization of the will*: the struggle against a despised part of the self is *displaced outward*, and is waged in the form of a struggle to destroy classes of persons which symbolize this despised part of the self.

3. The Struggle Against Passivity: Aurobindo

We have used the term *passivity* in this Chapter to refer, essentially, to a tendency existing within the individual which is the source of an *inability to encounter reality in an active, vigorous manner.* Passivity, according to this view, is experienced as a *force of inertia*, as an immense psychological "weight" which prevents the individual from penetrating into reality.

We may summarize previous discussion relating to this issue by suggesting that the sense of passivity is rooted, on the one hand, in the *sadism of the super-ego*, which creates an enormous psychic pressure "from above;" and is rooted, on the other hand, in the *masochism of the ego*, which creates an enormous psychic "drag," from below. In any case, it would appear, the impact of these intrapsychic forces is to effect a *diminuition in the power of the will.*

If there are forces within the individual which work to create a sense of passivity, there are other forces, however, in my view, which work *in opposition* to the passive tendencies, forces which compel the individual to move "upward and outward," *toward* the active encounter with reality.

Thus, given these competing intrapsychic tendencies, one may postulate the existence of a conflict within each and every human being: a conflict between the *active wish to encounter reality,* on the one hand; and the *passive wish to avoid the encounter with reality*, on the other.

We shall argue, here, that the revolutionary impulse grows out of the conflict between these active and passive wishes. Specifically, we wish to hypothesize that the revolutionary impulse develops where the passive tendency is *extremely powerful*; and where this tendency is experienced simultaneously, in a profound way, to be *ego-alien*; that the revolutionary struggle, in short, is a reflection of the individual's struggle to *liberate himself from his own passivity.*

According to this view, then, *political* struggles for liberation, struggles for liberation which are waged on the level of social reality, are a manifestation of this *intrapsychic* struggle for liberation: the struggle for liberation from a sadistic super-ego is transformed into a struggle for liberation from a sadistic "oppressor;" the struggle for liberation from one's own masochism is transformed into a struggle to "free the people" from their weaknesses and their downtrodden condition.

In the case of Aurobindo, I believe, one may observe this transformation; one may observe, that is to say, the manner in which perceptions rooted in the *intrapsychic* struggle for liberation are transformed into perceptions relating to the *political* struggle for liberation.

The following passages, for example, in which Aurobindo describes the effort which he believes is necessary if British oppression is to be resisted, reflect, in my view, a projected perception of the nature of the effort which is perceived to be necessary to resist a *sadistic super-ego*:

> We have seen Ramamurti . . . lie motionless, resistant, with a superhuman force of will power acting through the muscles, while two cars loaded with men are driven over his body. India must undergo an ordeal of passive endurance far more terrible without relaxing a single fibre of her frame.
>
> (Mukherjee, 1964, p. 346)

> We have seen Ramamurti break over his chest a strong iron chain tightened round his whole body and break it by the sheer force of will working through the body. India must work a similar deliverance for herself by the same inner force.
>
> (Mukherjee, 1964, pp. 346–347)

In other words, according to this view, it is the *sadistic super-ego* which is experienced by Aurobindo as "two cars driven over the body" and as an "iron chain tightened round the body." And it is the need to resist the super-ego which is perceived to require a "superhuman force of will-power."

Similarly, I believe, the following description of India's weaknesses represents a projected perception of the *weakness which Aurobindo experiences within himself.*

> What strength will help (India) to shake off the weaknesses which have crowded in on her? How will she raise herself from the dust whom a thousand shackles bind down? Only the strength of a superhuman ideal, only the gigantic force of a superhuman will, only the vehemence of an effort which transcends all that man has done and approaches divinity.
>
> (Mukherjee, 1964, p. 346)

Thus, according to this view, it is the *masochism of Aurobindo's ego* which gives rise to his perception of India as being "bound down in the dust by a thousand shackles." And, once again, resistance to a posture of masochistic passivity is perceived to require a "gigantic force of superhuman will."

These passages give an accurate sense, I believe, of the enormous *power* of the intrapsychic forces which work to create a sense of passivity. And give an accurate sense, at the same time, of the enormity of the *will to resist* these intrapsychic forces.

It is precisely the interaction between these opposing intrapsychic forces, the interaction, that is to say, between *forces which create a sense of passivity*, and the *need to resist these forces* which is the fundamental source, in my view, of the "revolutionary struggle," and of the violent, hysterical quality of revolutionary behavior. According to this hypothesis, the violence and hysteria which are bound up with the revolutionary impulse is rooted in the *desperate struggle*, on the part of the revolutionary, to *resist those intrapsychic forces which push him into a posture of passivity.*

We suggested earlier that Hitler's emphasis upon "crime" and upon violence was rooted in his belief that such modes of activity constituted an effective means of waging the struggle against passivity. Extending this interpretation we may hypothesize that the *entire ideology and life style of the revolutionary*, with its emphasis upon *struggle, will, violence, activity*, etc., is rooted in this struggle against passivity.

The revolutionary, according to this view, is an individual who experiences *profound intrapsychic pressures which force him away from reality and into a posture of passivity*. Consequently, because of the depth of his passivity, he is unable to encounter reality as the average person does, on the basis of ordinary, goal-oriented activities.

At the same time, however, I believe, the revolutionary is an individual who possesses a *profound wish to contact, and to have an impact upon, reality*. He desperately wishes, consequently, to *overcome* his passive tendencies. And it is the *desperate quality of the struggle to overcome passivity* which is the source, in my view, of the "radical" quality of revolutionary ideology and behavior: the revolutionary is willing to engage in any activity, however extreme, however bizarre, if it is perceived to represent an opportunity to permit him to "break through" the weight of passivity, and to make contact with reality.

Chapter IV

THE SOCIAL PSYCHOLOGY OF NATIONALISM

1. The "National Community"

Sociologists have identified, as a fundamental transition in the modern world, the transition from a *Gemeinschaft* mode of social organization to a *Gesellschaft* mode of social organization. This is, essentially, the process of *urbanization*. What is of concern to us here is the shift which occurs in the *nature of the community* as a consequence of this transition.

The *Gemeinschaft* mode of social organization is embodied, typically, in the village, the tribe, the small town, and may be characterized in terms of the existence of *personal interaction and intimacy* among persons in the environment. Persons *know one another* on a personal basis; and it is *interaction among persons in the immediate environment* which defines the individual's relationship to the community.

The *Gesellschaft* mode of social organization, on the other hand, is embodied, typically, in the large city, and may be characterized in terms of the *absence of personal interaction and intimacy* which exists among persons in the environment. Persons, for the most part, *do not know one another on a personal level*; and interaction with persons in the environment does not serve to define a relationship to the community. The question becomes, therefore: What is the nature of the community under conditions of the *Gesellschaft* society?

The answer to this question lies, I believe, in the development of "the nation" as a substitute for the "physically present" community. According to this view, as man *extricates himself* from the tribe, from the village, from the community as defined by a specific physical locale, he comes to embrace a "national community."[1]

This "national community" differs, of course, in certain fundamental ways, from the community as it had existed in the *Gemeinschaft* society. In the first place, it would appear, the development of such a community brings about a shift in the nature of the "group" with which the individual identifies. As Kohn observes:

> Nationalism—our identification with the life and aspirations of uncounted millions whom we shall never know, with a territory which we shall never visit in its entirety—is qualitatively different from the love of family or of home surroundings. It is qualitatively akin to the love of humanity or of the whole earth. Both belong to what Nietzsche called (in *Thus Spoke Zarathustra*) *Fernstenliebe*, love of those far away, and which he distinguished from the *Nachstenliebe*, love of those near by.
> (1944, p. 9)

Silvert notes, similarly, that where this transition occurs

> the qualitative nature of the "in group" versus "out group" feeling is changed by the inclusion of entire collectivities of persons never to be seen by the individual, never to be conversed with, never to be physically touched.
> (1963, p. 23)

[1] A detailed study of this transition appears in Lerner, 1958.

Secondly, we may suggest, where this transition occurs, there is a shift in the nature of the "issues and events" with which persons identify. No longer is the individual concerned, merely, with "local issues" and with "local events." Rather, persons become interested in "national issues," and in "national events," and come to believe that these are of fundamental significance, even where they do not impact, in a direct way, upon one's own personal life.

Let us turn, at this point, using the American case as a model, to a more detailed examination of the concept of a "national community."

The national community is rooted, we may suggest, in that "world" of events, issues and personalities which is "brought to us" by the mass-media of communication, i.e., by radio, television, newspapers, etc. And it is the *shared attachment to this world*, among the citizens of a nation, which generates, I believe, the sense of a national community.

Thus, for example, according to this view, a major sports event is important in American culture, not because of the "real" impact of such an event, but by virtue of the fact that an *interest and involvement in this event is shared by large numbers of persons*. When persons return to work on a Monday morning, it is the Sunday afternoon sports event which, in the absence of more substantial shared experiences, creates a common frame-of-reference, and gives persons something to talk about. Such an event functions, in short, to *bind persons together to create the sense of a national community*.

Similarly, we may suggest, persons are bound together in a national community by virtue of a shared attachment to various "famous personalities." As Americans, for example, we may have never met personally men such as John

Wayne, Groucho Marx, Johnny Carson, Joe Nameth, etc. Yet we feel deeply that we "know" these men. And the fact that we *share* this sense of knowledge, and intimacy, serves to create a bond among us.

We may take this a step further: "famous personalities," we may suggest, come to play, in the *Gesellschaft* society, the role which had been played by "neighbors" in the *Gemeinschaft* society, i.e., they come to constitute our fundamental "secondary relationships." Thus, according to this view, the development of a national community embodies a *transformation in the nature of the individual's connection to the community*: where once the individual's connection to the community had been defined in terms of relationships with persons *present* in the immediate physical environment, now this connection is defined in terms of relationships with persons *not present* in the immediate physical environment.[2]

There are a number of important changes which are associated with this shift in the nature of community. One of the most important of these, perhaps, is that a national community may be more easily "turned off" than a physically present community. If one does not wish to "interact" with one's "friends" from the mass-media, one may turn off the television, stop reading newspapers, etc.

A physically present community, on the other hand, is not avoided so easily. Rather, as students of the *Gemeinschaft* society have observed, such a community tends to act in a powerful way, whether or not one wishes it to do so, to impose moral standards, define social conventions, etc.

[2] A central "paradigm" for this transformation, we may suggest, is the situation which exists on a bus or subway in a large city: persons ignore one another, maintain the greatest possible physical and social distance from one another, yet are *deeply involved in reading their newspapers*. The sense of emotional involvement, in short, has been shifted from persons who are "close," to persons who are "far away."

In short, we may suggest, a fundamental difference between the *Gemeinschaft* and the national community lies in the *extent to which the community tends to regulate and to control the behavior of the individuals who reside within it.*

We may extend this interpretation: It is precisely the wish for personal freedom, the wish to become *liberated from the psychology of the group*, which is the fundamental determinant, we may suggest, of the entire transition which we have been discussing here, the transition, that is, from the *Gemeinschaft* to the *Gesellschaft* society. According to this view the change which occurs on the level of the social structure is a response to an *inner psychological dynamic*; is a response, that is to say, to man's wish to be *free*, and his wish to create a social environment in which he will be able to maximize his individual potentialities, without interference by the group.

The fact that man wishes to become *liberated from the community* does not mean, however, that the needs which have compelled him to be *connected to the community* disappear. Rather, once having achieved liberation from the *Gemeinschaft* society, man is confronted, it would appear, with psychological problems revolving around the *fear of separation from the intimate community.*

The national community develops, I believe, as a response to these psychological problems, functioning, essentially, to *alleviate the anxiety associated with separation from the intimate community*. Specifically, we may hypothesize, the stream of words and images which flows from the mass-media functions to *keep the individual company*, and to create, for him, the illusion that he is *not alone*.

The "national community," then, according to the theory developed here, is a special kind of community which possesses its own, unique dynamics: it is a community which functions, simultaneously, to permit the individual to be *free* of the group, yet to provide the emotional sense of being *connected* to the group. The national community may be characterized, in short, as the *community under conditions of individuation.*

2. Totalitarianism

We have hypothesized, then, that the *Gesellschaft* society and the "national community" develop as related phenomena. According to this view men tend to gravitate away from the *Gemeinschaft* society, and toward the city, because they wish to be *free*, because they wish to become liberated from the shackles imposed by the group. While, at the same time, a symbolic community, "the nation," evolves as a *substitute* for the *Gemeinschaft* community, a substitute which is appropriate because, as we have observed, it functions to provide some of the *intimacy and sense of belonging* which had been provided by the *Gemeinschaft* society, but imposes few of its *restrictions*.

For many persons in contemporary societies, then, it would appear, the "urban/nationalism" solution is a satisfactory one: they pursue individualized lives, the locus of which is work and the family, and when they wish to participate in the "community," they watch television, or read the newspaper.

For others, however, we may suggest, such a mode of social life is unsatisfactory: the pleasures of individuality cannot compensate for the loss of the intimate community. And "the nation" is not an adequate substitute: it is too distant, too abstract, cannot provide the sense of "belonging" which the individual craves. For such persons, I believe, the *Gesellschaft* society is experienced, not as an opportunity for growth and for the development of individuality, but as the source of an *intolerable loss*.

It is my view that many of the "social movements" which characterize modern societies grow out of this sense of loss, and that they function, essentially, to provide a means by which the individual may "escape from freedom (Fromm, 1969);" that they develop, in short, as a response to the human desire to create a mode of social life which will permit persons to be *relieved of the burden of separateness and individuality*. I wish, here, to discuss one such social movement: the "totalitarian society."

As a means of introducing the totalitarian idea, let us present several passages from the writings of Karl Marx. What these passages demonstrate, I believe, is that at the heart of Marx's thinking lies a *hatred of the Gesellschaft society*; a hatred, that is to say, of a society which fosters the development of "separateness" among persons; and which encourages the individual to "do his own thing," apart from the community.

Marx observes, correctly I believe, that the idea of liberty is bound up with the right of men to *separate* from society, and from one another:

> Liberty as a right of man is not founded upon the relations between man and man, but rather upon the separation of man from man. It is the right of such separation. The right of the *circumscribed* individual, withdrawn into himself.
>
> (1964a, pp. 24–25)

> Man . . . as a member of civil society . . . (is) an individual separated from the community, withdrawn into himself, wholly preoccupied with his private interest and acting in accordance with his private caprice. Man is far from being considered, in the rights of man, as a species-being; on the contrary, species life itself–society–appears as a system which is external to the individual and as a limitation of his original independence.
>
> (1964a, p. 26)

The emergence of such a mode of social life, however, from Marx's point of view, is by no means a positive development:

> Human life is the true *social life* of man . . . the irremediable exclusion from this life is . . . more complete, more unbearable, dreadful and contradictory than the exclusion from political life.
> (in Bender, 1972, p. 236)

Rather, Marx believes, the right of persons to become "released from general shackles and the limitations imposed by man (1964b, p. 219)" is the "expression of (man's) absolute enslavement and . . . the loss of human nature (1964b, p. 219)." The true achievement of "human emancipation" will occur, according to Marx, only when

> the real, individual man has absorbed into himself the abstract citizen; when as an individual man, in his everyday life, in his work, and in his relationships, he has become a *species-being.*
> (1964a, p. 31)

It is clear, then, that Marx's concept of "emancipation" is quite different from the manner in which it is ordinarily conceived. Emancipation, for Marx, lies not in the individual's capacity to become "released from the shackles" which are imposed by the state, but in precisely the opposite situation: in man's capacity to "absorb into himself the abstract citizen."

This concept of emancipation is not, however, idiosyncratic to Marx: it is a central element in the tradition of nationalism as well. Thus Kedourie (1960), tracing the history of nationalism, discusses a similar "metaphysical" theory of the relationship between the individual and the state as it developed in the early nineteenth century. He cites F.W. Schelling:

> The freedom of the individual, which is his self-realization, lies in identifying himself with the whole, belonging to which endows him with reality. Complete freedom means total absorption in the whole, and the story of human freedom consists in the progressive struggle to reach this end.
>
> (p. 29)

And Adam Muller:

> (The state is) the totality of human affairs, their union into a living whole. If we exclude for ever from this association even the most unimportant part of the human being, if we separate private life from public life even at only one point, then we can no longer perceive the state as a phenomenon of life, or as an idea.
>
> (p. 39)

According to Muller the alienation within man could not be abolished

> so long as state and citizen serve two masters . . . so long as hearts are internally rent by a double desire, the one to live as a citizen in a state . . . the other, to extract himself from the whole civil order, to cut himself off from that same state along with his domestic and private life.
>
> (p. 46)

The development of the modern nation-state is dependent, I believe, upon the acceptance of the proposition that *one's own fate and destiny is intimately linked with the fate and destiny of the nation*. What occurs in the case of men such as Marx, Schelling and Muller, therefore, we may suggest, is that this idea is *carried to its logical extreme.* These men, in other words, would appear to embrace the notion that the fate of the individual and the fate of the nation are *entirely* bound together; that there is no such thing as a *private* sphere, a sphere of reality in which men pursue goals which are *unrelated* to the state.

It is my view, then, that at the heart of the totalitarian idea lies a tendency toward the *denial of a sphere of reality which is separate from the state.* The totalitarian tends to believe that *the community is everything*: that human activities are meaningful and worthwhile only when performed in the name of the state.[3]

This tendency, the tendency toward the *denial of a sphere of reality which is separate from the state*, is a central theme in Lenin's ideology. I wish to briefly examine this theme, here, as it appears in Lenin's writings.

Lenin experienced an extraordinary amount of hostility toward "the state" (see especially Lenin, 1970). And a fundamental source of this hostility, it would appear, lie in Lenin's perception of the state as a structure which stood "above" society; in his perception of the state as a structure which was *separate and distinct* from the great mass of persons.[4] One of Lenin's central goals as a revolutionary, therefore, was the *destruction of the state*; the destruction, that is to say, of this "alien structure" which separated the people from the government.

The ultimate achievement of this goal, from the communist point of view, would take place upon the occasion of the "withering away of the state," that is, upon the occasion of the complete *disappearance* of the state structure. In the meantime, however, Lenin conceived of a kind of state in which, at least, the most objectionable characteristics of the state would be eliminated. Specifically, Lenin con-

[3]It is for this reason, I believe, that the idea of *capitalism* is in fundamental opposition to the idea of totalitarianism. The capitalist pursues a *private* aspiration; wishes to do something *for himself*; and therefore contradicts, in his attitude and his behavior, the proposition that human activities are worthwhile only when pursued in the name of the community.

[4]Thus Lenin describes the state, typically, as "a power standing *above* society and increasingly alienating itself from it (1970, p. 9)." And asks: "What is it that places (officials) *above* society (1970, p. 14)?"

ceived of a form of the state in which *the great mass of persons would take part in the running of the government.* Lenin describes this concept of the state, typically, as follows:

> Instead of the special institutions of a privileged minority (privileged officialdom, the chiefs of the standing army), the majority itself can directly fulfill all these functions, and the more the functions of the state power devolve upon the people as a whole the less need is there for the existence of this power.
> (1970, pp. 50–51)

Describes a moment, early in the revolution, when he believes this concept has been actualized:

> Our new state is *no longer* a state in the proper sense of the term, for in some parts of Russia these contingents of armed men are the *masses themselves*, the entire people, and not certain privileged individuals placed over the people, and divorced from the people.
> (1964a, p. 85)

And speaks, finally, of setting up "a state apparatus consisting of ten if not twenty million people (1964b, p. 114)."

Insofar as the "majority of the people perform state functions," the state, indeed, has ceased to exist in the sense of being a structure which is *separate and distinct* from the great mass of persons. Rather, under such circumstances, *the state and the people have become one and the same.*

The logic of this idea, the logic, that is to say, of a state which simultaneously *does not exist* and which *consists of the entire citizenry* is contained, I believe, in the following passage from one of Stalin's speeches:

> We stand for the withering away of the state. At the same time we stand for the strengthening of the dictatorship of the proletariat, which represents the most powerful and mighty form of the state which has existed up to the present day.
> (quoted in McNeal, 1963, p. 104)

Commenting upon this passage, McNeal suggests that it may reflect, "however awkwardly"[5]

> the truly totalitarian belief that the state can become nothing only by becoming everything, by engulfing individual identity to the point at which the state is no longer distinguishable from mankind.
>
> (1963, p. 104)

The conception of society which is put forth by Lenin and by Stalin, then, is entirely consistent with the totalitarian ideal as defined by the writers cited above.[6] It is a conception of society in which *all of social reality is identified with the state.* We may pose the question, therefore: What is the psychological function of such a conception of social reality?

The totalitarian conception of social reality functions, I believe, as a means of *denying the reality of separateness.* For if one accepts the central premise of totalitarianism—that there is no such thing as a sphere of reality which is separate from the community—then it follows logically that there can be no such thing as an *individual* who is separate from the community; that there can be no such thing, in short, as an

[5]Haimson observes, similarly, that "With the one-party state that Lenin founded, he strove, and Stalin strove more successfully, to embrace every aspect of social and individual life, until the party and its state became, or sought to become, co-extensive with society, thereby swelling to totality. In place of every cook becoming master of affairs of state, the state became master of the affairs of every cook (1969, p. 37)."

[6]As is the conception of society put forth by the Nazis. Thus, Stuckart and Globke describe the "volk community" as follows: "The community of the volk is the primary value in the life of the whole as well as of the individual . . . National Socialism does not recognize a separate individual sphere which, apart from the community, is to be painstakingly protected from any interference by the state. The moral personality can prove itself only within the community. Every activity of daily life has meaning and value only as a service to the whole . . . In the legal order, therefore, the position of the individual is no longer determined in terms of the person as such, but in terms of the community (quoted in Mosse, 1968, p. 330)."

"alienated" human being, a human being who is cut off from society, and from his fellow-man.

We suggested earlier that the acceptance of separateness and of individuality, the acceptance of the *Gesellschaft* society, is facilitated, for modern man, by virtue of the development of a "national community," a community which functions to alleviate anxiety, and to provide a sense of security.

For the totalitarian, however, it would appear, such a "compromise solution" is perceived to be inadequate. That is to say: the totalitarian may be characterized as an individual who finds the experience of separateness, the experience of the *Gesellschaft* society, to be so intolerable that he is willing to take whatever measures are necessary to *abolish* such an experience.

And the analysis presented here suggests that one of the totalitarian's central efforts in the direction of achieving this goal takes the form of an effort to *create and to embrace an omnipotent community*. The totalitarian, in other words, wishes to create a community which is so powerful and so all-embracing that, in the face of such a community, it will be *impossible to perceive that the individual exists as an entity which is separate and distinct from the community.*[7]

3. The Renunciation of Personal Gratification in the Name of a Devotion to the Collectivity

It is within the framework of this desire to create and to

[7]The totalitarian, from this point of view (see also Chapter I), may be characterized as an individual who wishes to *actualize the image of the omnipotent mother in the nation*, an omnipotent mother which functions, not only to provide comfort and security, but to *destroy those who would become separate from her*. In his fear of separation and individuality, the totalitarian, I believe, *embraces* the destructive aspects of the omnipotent mother, encourages her to "swallow up" her children.

embrace an omnipotent community that one may understand, I believe, the tendency, so common among nationalists, revolutionaries and totalitarians toward "sacrifice;" the tendency, that is to say, toward the *renunciation of personal gratification in the name of a devotion to the collectivity.*[8] Let us begin our analysis of this tendency by examining an incident from Hitler's life.

When asked why he would not marry Eva Braun Hitler reportedly replied that "He could not . . . love Germany and a wife at the same time (Snyder, 1961, p. 167)." In the last day of his life, however, when Germany's destruction is assured, Hitler consents to become married. Shirer (1959) explains Hitler's reasoning:

> He has always said that marriage would interfere with his complete dedication to leading first his party to power and then his nation to the heights. Now that there was no more leading to do and his life was at an end, he could safely enter into a marriage which could last only a few hours.
>
> (pp. 1457–1458)

Hitler's attitude, then, is reminiscient of St. Paul's explanation for his belief that a true Christian should not marry: "A man who is married cannot have much energy left over for God." What is implied, in each case, is that an ascetic posture toward women is necessary if one wishes to do justice to one's devotion to a "higher" love-object, God in the case of St. Paul, Germany in the case of Hitler.

The tendency toward renunciation, then, we may suggest, may be characterized as a *shift in the distribution of the libido*: libido which had been directed toward *gratifi-*

[8]This tendency is expressed, typically, in Mao's statement that a communist should "subordinate (his personal interests) to the interests of the nation and of the masses (1971, p. 42);" and in his statement that a communist should "be more concerned about the Party and the masses than about any individual, and more concerned about others than about himself (1971, pp. 136–137)."

cation in reality comes to be attached to an *omnipotent collectivity*, and leads to the wish to "serve" this omnipotent collectivity.

It is the *conflict* between these tendencies, the conflict, that is to say, between the wish to *pursue gratification in reality* and the wish to *embrace an omnipotent collectivity* which is one of the central themes, it would appear, of Freud's *Civilization and its Discontents* (1962). Freud states, typically:

> The most important thing is the aim of creating a unity out of the individual human beings. It is true that the aim of happiness is still there, but it is pushed into the background. It almost seems as if the creation of a great human community would be most successful if no attention had to be paid to the happiness of the individual.
>
> (p. 87)

What we have described, then, as a tendency toward renunciation in the name of the collectivity, Freud describes as a tendency toward foregoing happiness in the name of the creation of a "great human community." We may pose, therefore, the following question: What is the source of this tendency?

Freud would appear to be unable to provide a definitive explanation. At one point he suggests that the tendency of the libido to "expand" to embrace a great human community is inherently the "work of Eros:"

> Civilization is a process in the service of Eros, whose purpose is to combine single human individuals, and after that families, then races, peoples and nations into one great unity, the unity of mankind. Why this has to happen, we don't know; the work of Eros is precisely this. These collections of men are to be libidinally bound to one another.
>
> (1962, p. 69)

In another place, however, Freud indicates that, under certain circumstances, the libido *will not* exhibit a tendency to expand:

> Sexual love is a relationship between two individuals in which a third can only be superfluous or disturbing, whereas civilization depends on relationships between a considerable number of individuals. When a love-relationship is at its height there is no room left for any interest in the environment; a pair of lovers are sufficient to themselves, and do not even need the child they have in common to make them happy. In no other case does Eros so clearly betray the core of his being, the purpose of making one out of more than one; but when he has achieved this in the proverbial way through the love of two human beings, he refuses to go further.
>
> (1962, p. 55)

Thus, if this observation is correct, the tendency of the libido to expand to embrace a great human community is not inherently "the work of Eros."

Our own explanation for the "expansive" tendency of the libido has been suggested in earlier discussions (see especially Chapter I). Our view is, essentially, that the human desire to create a "great human community" has its source in the *striving for narcissistic omnipotence*, a striving which takes the form, in this instance, of a desire to *create and to merge with an omnipotent community*. Let us examine this motive, here, in greater detail.

Human beings would appear to find it difficult to renounce the dream of infantile omnipotence. Put another way: they would appear to find it difficult to face the reality of the "smallness" of their lives; to face the perception of the relative insignificance of human existence.

And one of the ways in which human beings attempt to compensate for the sense of the "smallness" of their lives, we may suggest, is through the creation of *omnipotent collectivities*, e.g., "big" countries; "powerful" states; "great masses of people," etc. Insofar as the individual identifies with these collectivities, he may partake of their "bigness," and thus may "recapture" a sense of his lost omnipotence.

It is our view, then, that the omnipotent nation/state functions to permit the persons who reside within it to recover a sense of omnipotence. The extent to which the nation is actually *used* to gratify this need would, of course, vary from individual to individual. For most persons in contemporary societies, we may suggest, there exists a relative "balance" between a devotion to the collectivity, on the one hand, and the pursuit of private aspirations, on the other.

What occurs in the case of the intensely committed nationalist, revolutionary or totalitarian, however, I believe, is that this "balance" is upset: *the wish to serve the collectivity becomes the central goal in life*, and individualized, personal aspirations are pushed into the background.

Men such as these, we may hypothesize, are men who find it *particularly difficult to renounce the dream of omnipotence*. They are men who find the idea of a small, "bourgeois" life, of a life in which each individual pursues his own modest aspirations, to be *particularly intolerable*.

Rather, we may suggest, for men such as these, the only life worth living is a "big" life. And they strive to create a sense of "bigness" in their lives by *identifying with omnipotent collectivities* and by *pursuing grandiose aspirations in relation to these collectivities* (e.g., serving the state, saving the people, etc.).

A fundamental source of the human desire to create a "great human community," then, according to the theory presented here, lies in the *refusal to abandon the dream of omnipotence*. It is in the name of the perpetuation of this dream, I believe, that man will "sacrifice" his freedom, his individuality, and his humanity.

BIBLIOGRAPHY

Arendt, H. *On Revolution.* New York: The Viking Press, 1971

Aurobindo, S. *Speeches.* Pondicherry: Sri Aurobindo Ashram, 1952a

Aurobindo, S. *The Doctrine of Passive Resistance.* Pondicherry: Sri Aurobindo Ashram, 1952b

Aurobindo, S. *On Nationalism.* Pondicherry: Sri Aurobindo Ashram, 1965

Baynes, N. H. *The Speeches of Adolf Hitler,* April 1922-August 1939. Two volumes. New York: Oxford University Press, 1942

Bender, F. L., Editor. Karl Marx: *Essential Writings.* New York: Harper Torchbooks, 1972

Brown, N. O. *Life Against Death.* Middletown, Connecticut: Wesleyan University Press, 1959

Djilas, M. *Conversations with Stalin.* New York: Harcourt, Brace and World, 1962

Fichte, J. G. *Addresses to the German Nation.* New York: Harper Torchbooks, 1968

Franklin, B., Editor. *The Essential Stalin: Major Theoretical Writings,* 1905-52. New York: Doubleday, 1972

Freud, S. *Civilization and Its Discontents.* New York: W. W. Norton, 1962

Fromm, E. *Escape from Freedom.* New York: Discus Books, 1969

Haimson, L. H. *The Russian Marxists and the Origins of Bolshevism.* Cambridge, Mass.: Harvard University Press, 1967

Hitler, A. *Mein Kampf.* Boston: Houghton Mifflin Company, 1962

Kedourie, E. *Nationalism.* London: Hutchinson, 1960

Kedourie, E. *Nationalism in Asia and Africa.* New York: World Publishing Company, 1970

Koenigsberg, R. A. *Hitler's Ideology: A Study in Psychoanalytic Sociology.* New York: The Library of Social Science, 1975

Kohn, H. *The Idea of Nationalism.* New York: The Macmillan Company, 1944

Kohn, H. *Prophets and Peoples.* New York: The Macmillan Company, 1952

Kubizek, A. *Young Hitler: The Story of our Friendship.* London: Allan Wingate, 1954

Lenin, V. I. *Collected Works.* Volume 9. Moscow: Foreign Languages Press, 1962a

Lenin, V. I. *Collected Works.* Volume 12. Moscow: Foreign Languages Press, 1962b

Lenin, V. I. *Collected Works.* Volume 24. Moscow: Progress Publishers, 1964a

Lenin, V. I. *Collected Works.* Volume 26. Moscow: Progress Publishers, 1964b

Lenin, V. I. *The Proletarian Revolution and the Renegade Kautsky.* Peking: Foreign Languages Press, 1965a

Lenin, V. I. *Two Tactics of Social Democracy in the Democratic Revolution.* Peking: Foreign Languages Press, 1965b

Lenin, V. I. *Collected Works.* Volume 33. Moscow: Progress Publishers, 1966

Lenin, V. I. *The State and Revolution.* Peking: Foreign Languages Press, 1970

Lerner, D. *The Passing of Traditional Society.* New York: Free Press, 1958

Marx, K. *Early Writings.* New York: McGraw-Hill, 1964a

Marx, K. *Selected Writings in Sociology and Social Philosophy.* New York: McGraw-Hill, 1964b

McNeal, R. H. *The Bolshevik Tradition.* Englewood, N.J.: Prentice-Hall, 1963

Mao-Tsetung. *Selected Readings.* Peking: Foreign Languages Press, 1971

Meyer, F. S. *The Moulding of Communists.* New York: Harcourt, Brace and World, 1961

Michelet, J. *The People.* New York: D. Appleton and Company, 1846

Michelet, J. *History of the French Revolution.* Chicago: University of Chicago Press, 1967

Minogue, K. R. *Nationalism.* New York: Basic Books, 1967

Mosse, G. L., Editor. *Nazi Culture.* New York: Grosset and Dunlap, 1968

Mukherjee, H. and Mukherjee, U., Editors. *Sri Aurobindo and the New Thought in Indian Politics.* Calcutta: K. L. Mukhopaahyay, 1964

Payne, R. *The Rise and Fall of Stalin.* New York: Avon Books, 1966

Payne, R. *The Life and Death of Lenin.* New York: Avon Books, 1967

Petrarch. *Sonnets and Songs.* New York: Grosset and Dunlop, 1968

Rauschning, H. *The Voice of Destruction.* New York: G. P. Putnam's Sons, 1940

Rigby, T. H., Editor. *Stalin: Great Lives Observed.* Englewood Cliffs, N.J.: Prentice-Hall, 1972

Roussy de Sales, R., Editor. *My New Order.* New York: Reynal and Hitchcock, 1941

Sartre, J. P. *Anti-Semite and Jew.* New York: Schocken Books, 1969

Schapiro, L. and Reddaway, P., Editors. *Lenin: The Man, the Theorist, the Leader: A Reappraisal.* New York: Frederick A. Praeger, 1967

Shafer, B. C. *Faces of Nationalism.* New York: Harcourt Brace Jovanovich, 1972

Shirer, W. L. *The Rise and Fall of the Third Reich.* New York: Simon and Schuster, 1959

Silverman, S. N., Editor. *Lenin: Great Lives Observed.* Englewood Cliffs, N.J.: Prentice-Hall, 1972

Silvert, K. H., Editor. *Expectant Peoples: Nationalism and Development.* New York: Vintage Books, 1963

Singh, K. *Prophet of Indian Nationalism: A Study of the Political Thought of Sri Aurobindo Ghosh.* London: Allen and Unwin, 1963

Snyder, L. *Hitler and Nazism.* New York: Franklin Watts, 1961

Speer, A. *Inside the Third Reich.* New York: The Macmillan Company, 1970

Stalin, J. *Selected Writings.* New York: International Publishers, 1942

Valentinov, N. *Encounters with Lenin.* London: Oxford University Press, 1968

Valentinov, N. *The Early Years of Lenin.* Ann Arbor: The University of Michigan Press, 1969

Von Maltitz, H. *The Evolution of Hitler's Germany.* New York: McGraw-Hill, 1973

Wolfe, B. D. *An Ideology in Power.* New York: Stein and Day, 1969

INDEX

9 781593 118570

Printed and bound by CPI Group (UK) Ltd, Croydon, CR0 4YY
15/09/2026
14962367-0004